RECORDED VERSIONS GUITAR

AUTHENTIC TRANSCRIPTIONS
WITH NOTES AND TABLATURE

THE BEST OF DICK DALE

M000159218

Music transcriptions by Pete Billmann and Jeff Jacobson

ISBN 0-634-06468-1

HAL•LEONARD® CORPORATION

7777 W. BLUEMOUND RD. P.O. BOX 13819 MILWAUKEE, WI 53213

Visit Hal Leonard Online at
www.halleonard.com

from *Better Shred Than Dead – The Dick Dale Anthology*

Banzai Washout

Words and Music by Steve Douglas

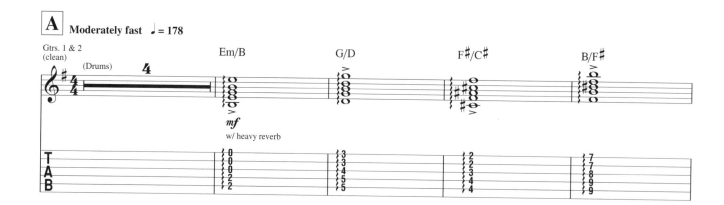

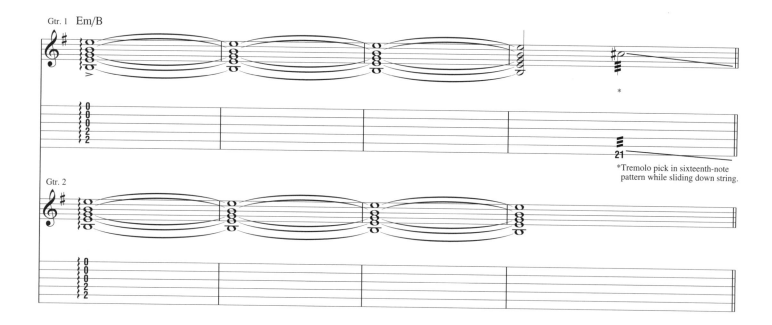

*Tremolo pick in sixteenth-note pattern while sliding down string.

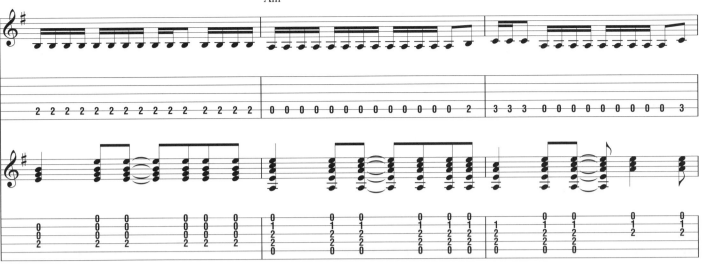

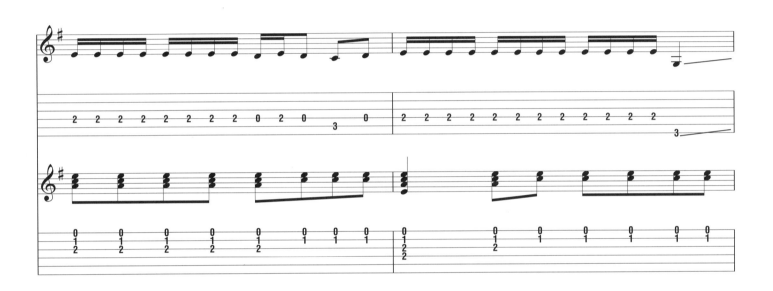

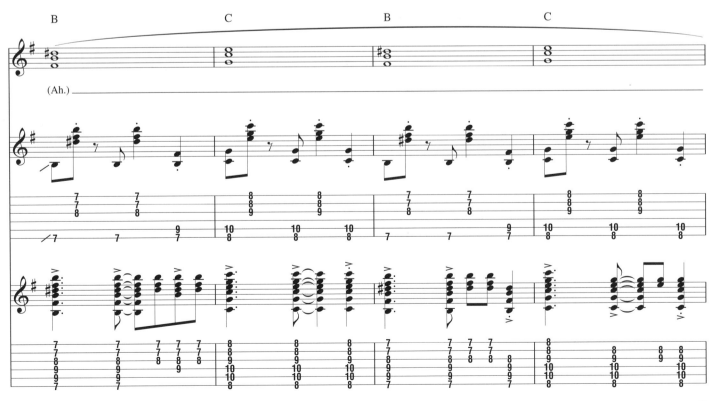

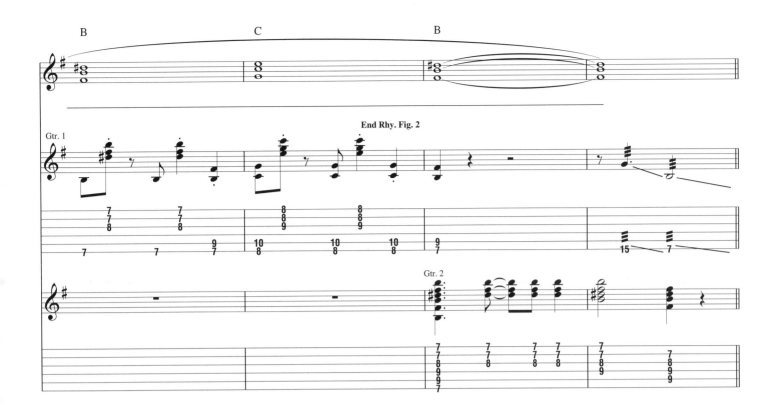

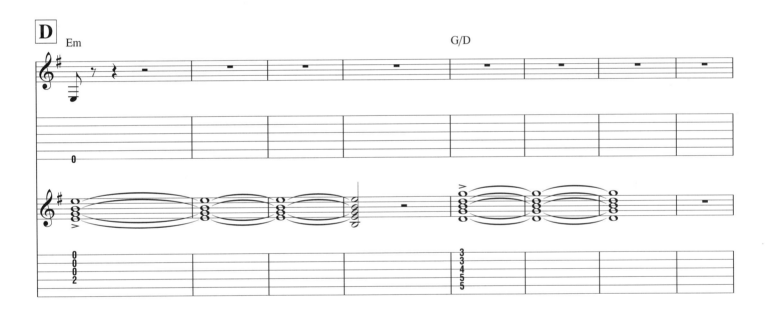

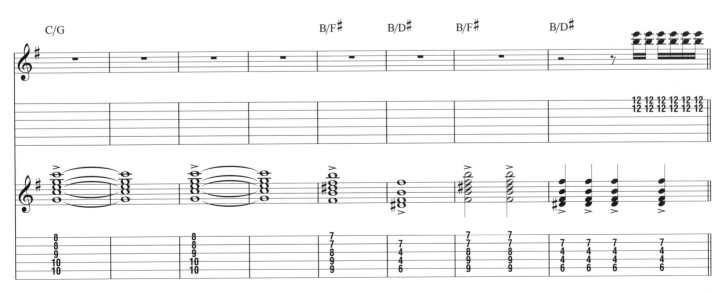

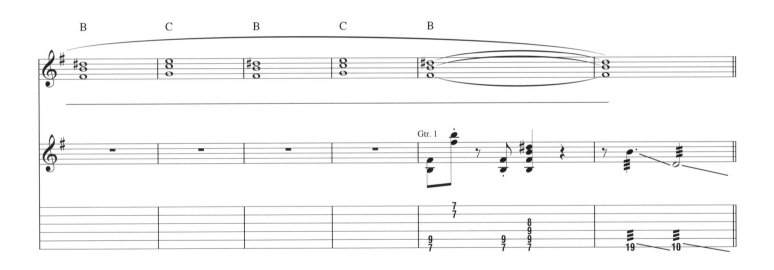

Begin fade

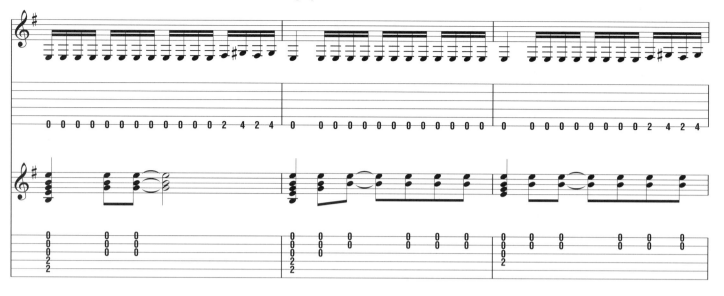

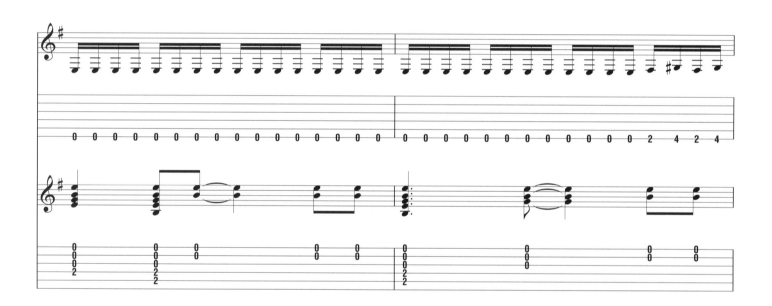

Fade out

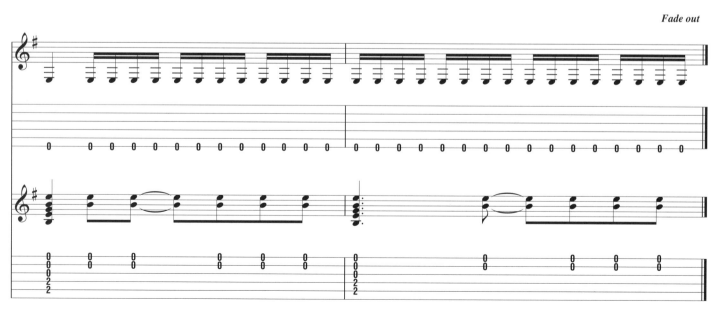

from Dick Dale – *Tribal Thunder*

The Eliminator

By Dick Dale

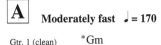

Moderately fast ♩ = 170

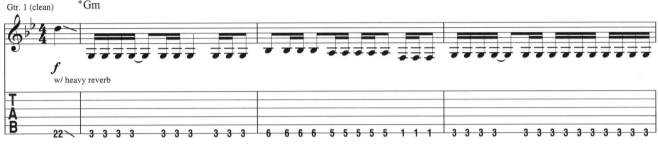

*Chord symbols reflect implied harmony.

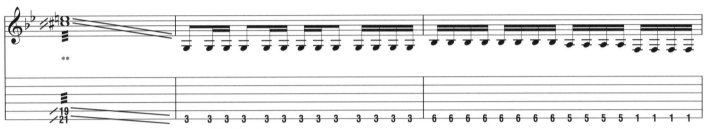

**Tremolo pick in sixteenth-note pattern while sliding down strings.

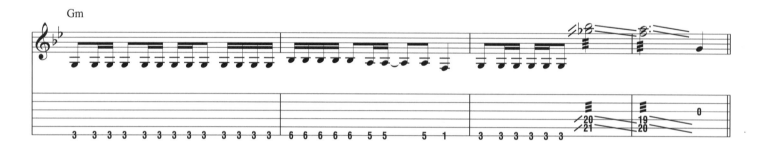

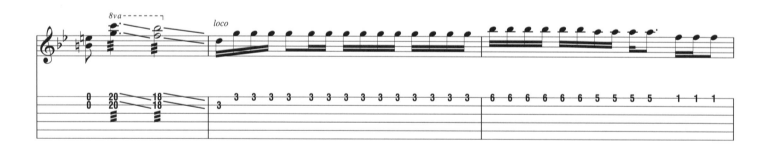

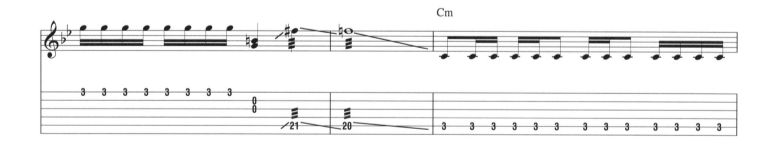

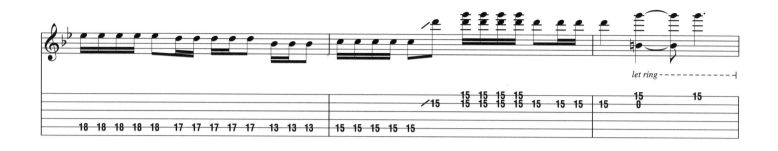

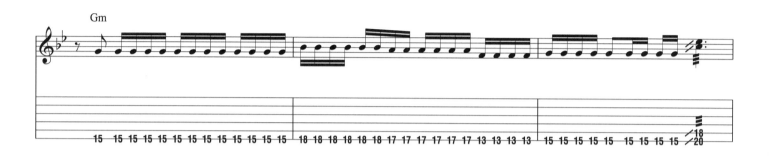

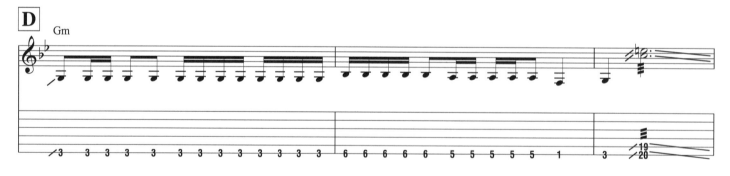

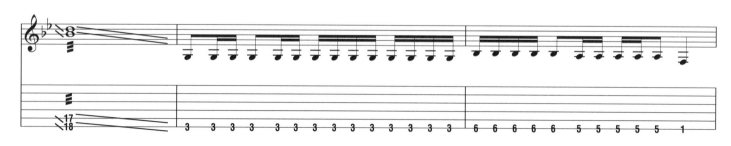

from Dick Dale – *Tribal Thunder*

Esperanza

By Dick Dale

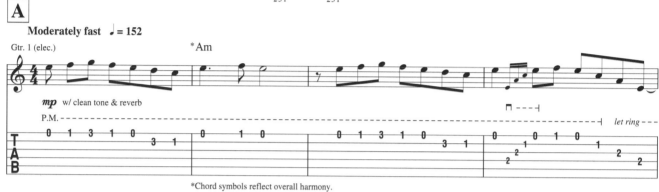

*Chord symbols reflect overall harmony.

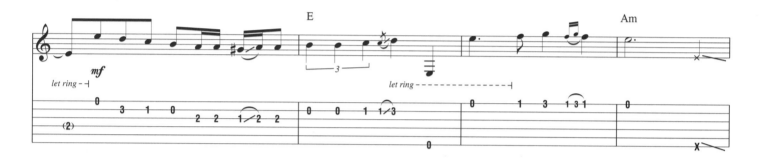

**Tremolo pick in sixteenth-note
pattern while sliding down strings.

*Delay set for eighth-note regeneration w/ 2 repeats.

Hava Nagila

Traditional
Arranged by Dick Dale

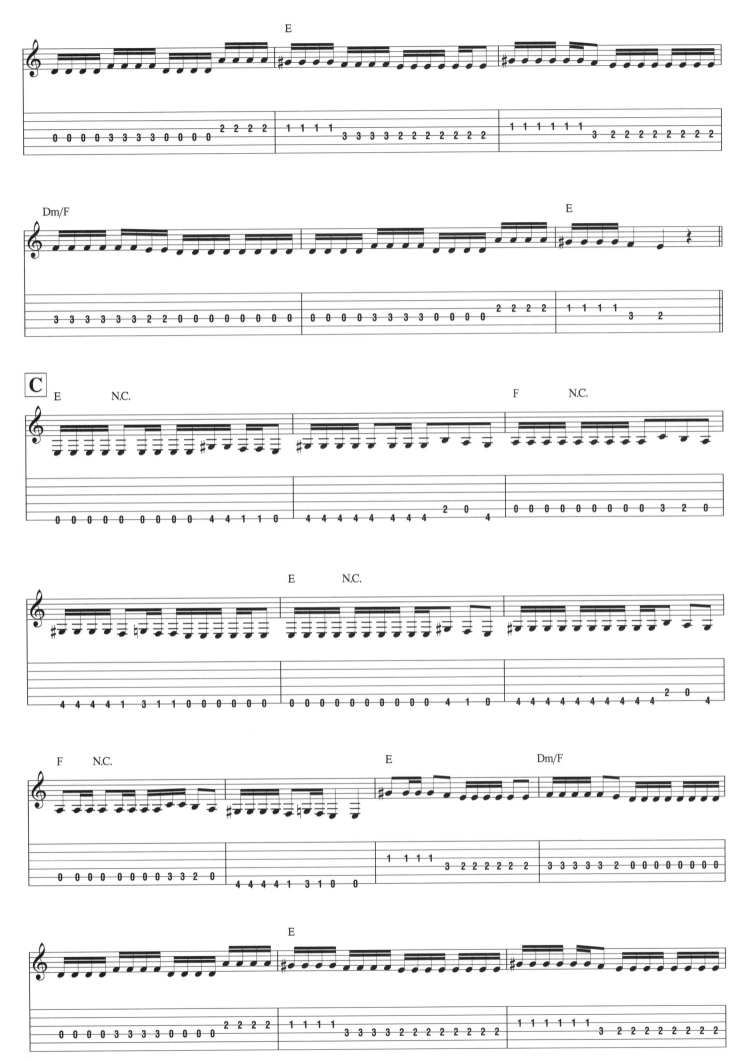

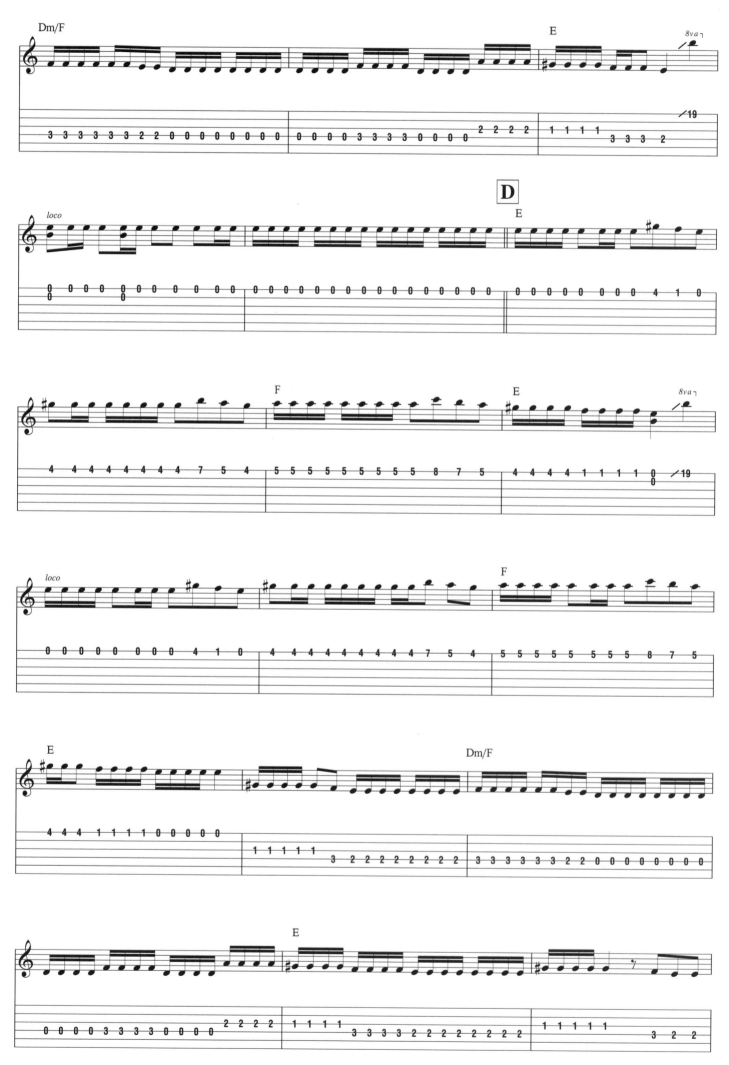

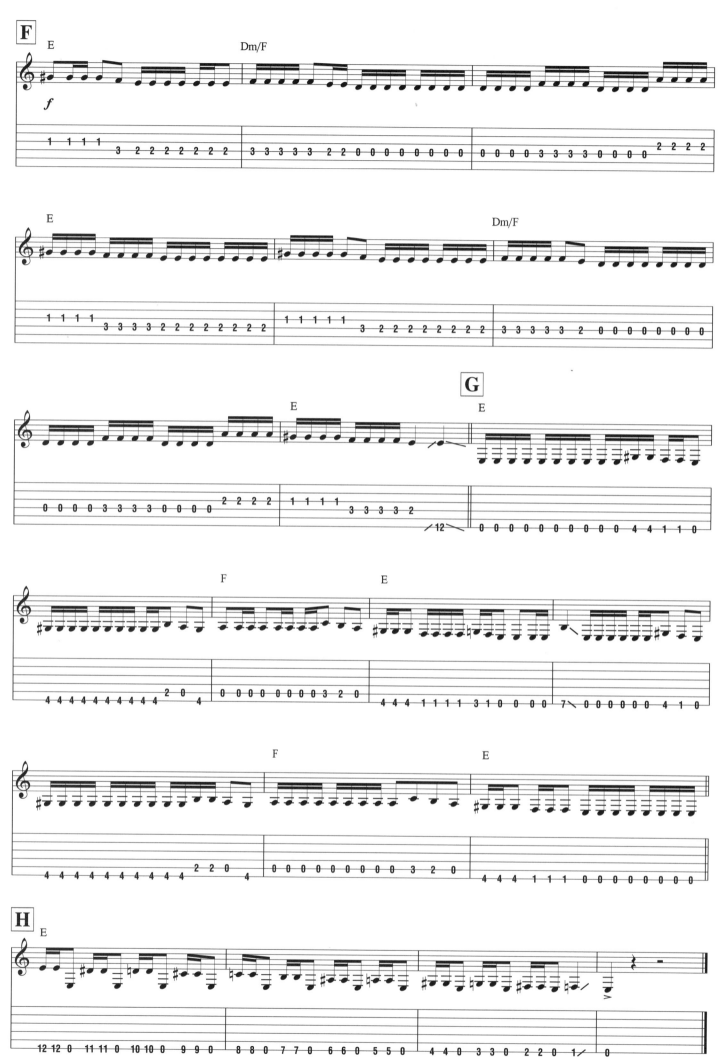

HMFIC

By Dick Dale

E5   E

A **Moderately fast** ♩ = 164

*E5

Shouted: HMFIC!

Gtr. 1 (dist.)

*Chord symbols reflect overall harmony.

Gtr. 2
(dist.)

B ⑥ 19 fr   E ⑥ open

mp

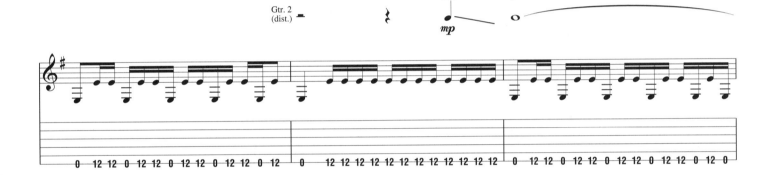

(cont. in notation)

Gtrs. 1 & 2

**

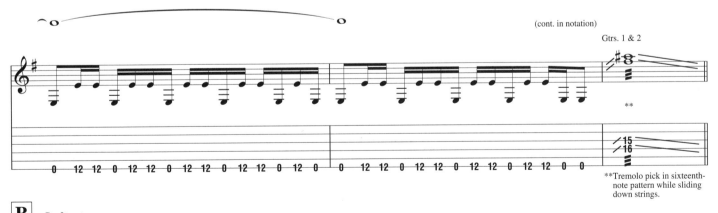

**Tremolo pick in sixteenth-note pattern while sliding down strings.

B Gtr. 2 tacet

Gtr. 1   E5

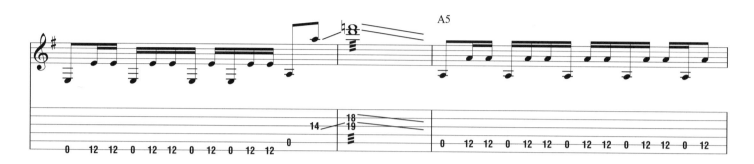

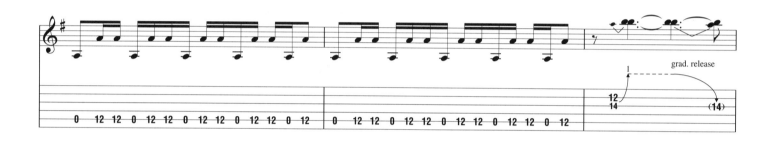

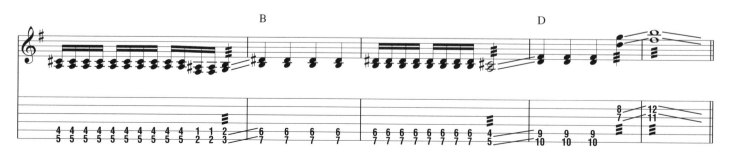

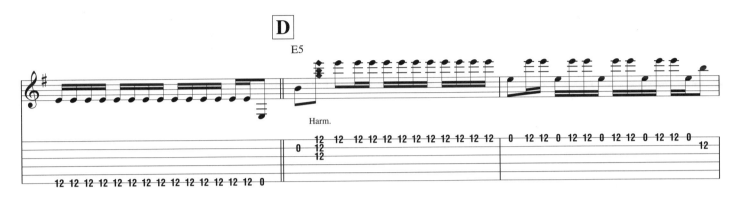

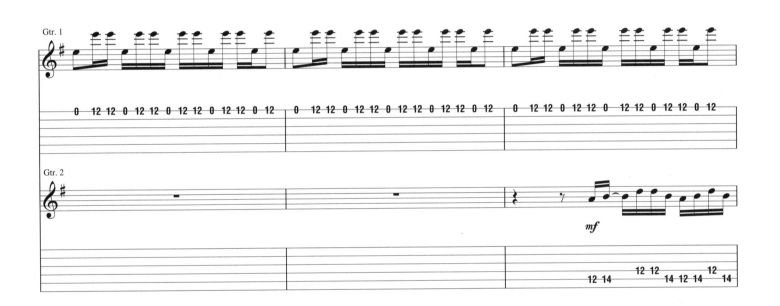

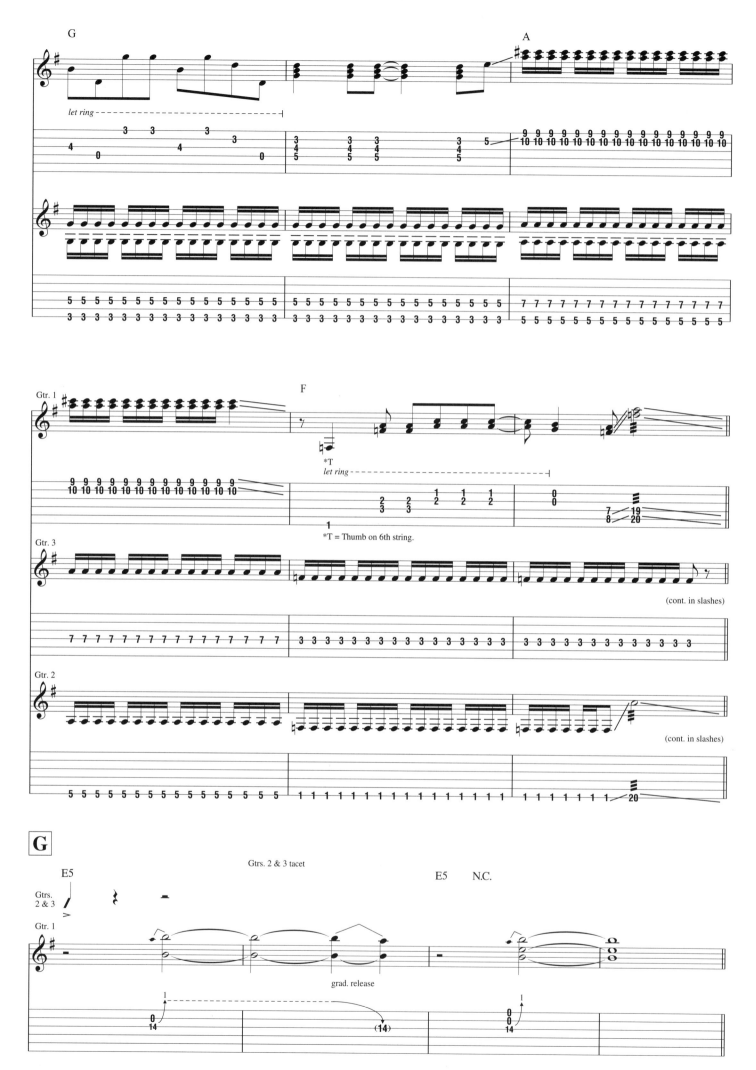

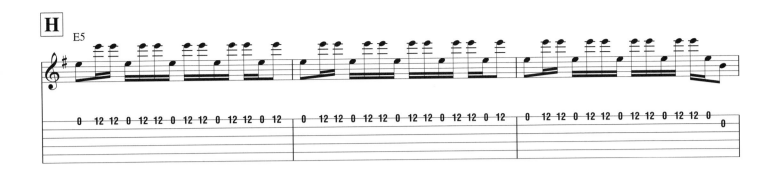

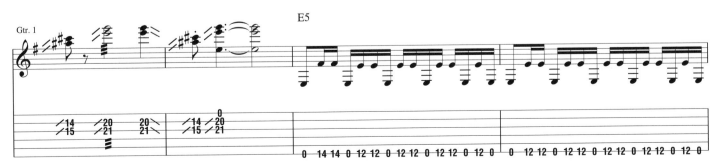

Gtr. 3: w/ Rhy. Fig. 1 (2 times)

*Gtr. 3

*Till end of song, all chords played by Gtr. 3 are generated by reverse delay.
**w/ vol. pedal or knob

K Gtr. 3: w/ Rhy. Fig. 1 (10 times)

steady gliss.

loco

steady gliss.

steady gliss.

Gtr. 3

loco

***w/ vol. pedal

33

King of the Surf Guitar

By Alonzo B. Willis

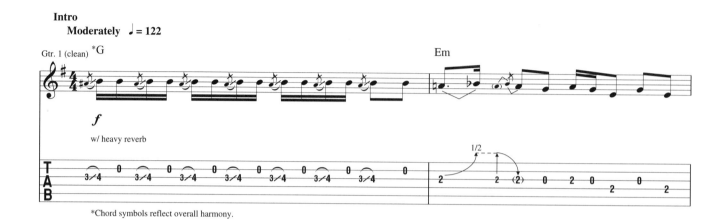

*Chord symbols reflect overall harmony.

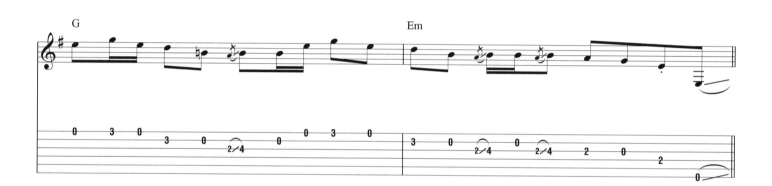

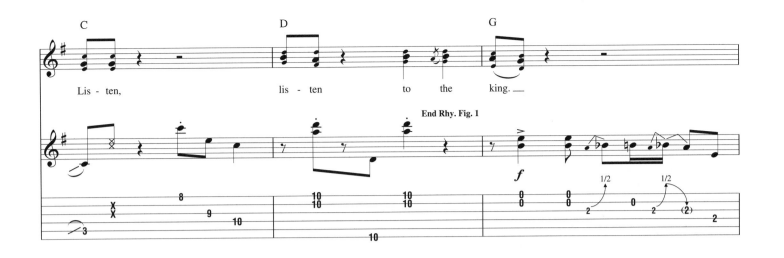

Lis - ten,   lis - ten to the king. ___

End Rhy. Fig. 1

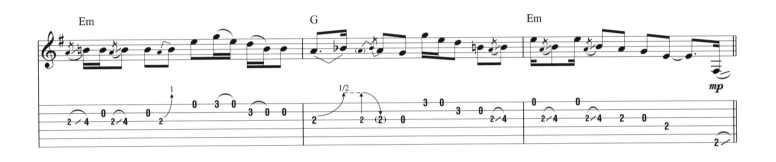

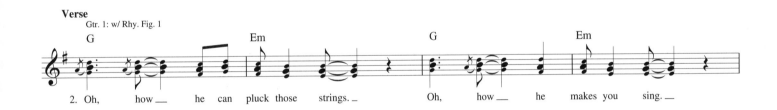

Verse

Gtr. 1: w/ Rhy. Fig. 1

2. Oh, how ___ he can pluck those strings. ___   Oh, how ___ he makes you sing. ___

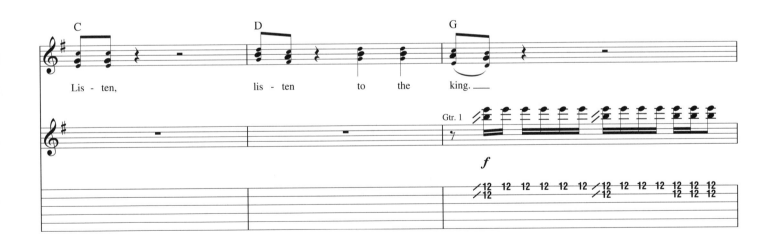

Lis - ten,   lis - ten to the king. ___

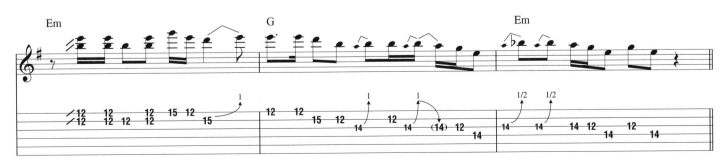

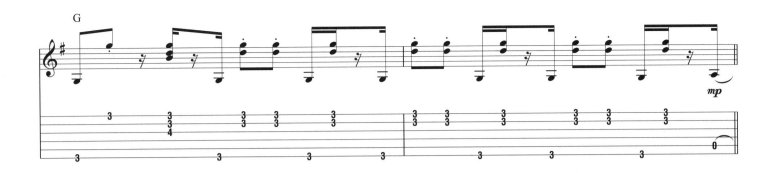

Chorus

From Beau-mont to An-a-heim, ___ San Ber-nar-di-no to Riv-er-side, ___

all the kids in all L. A. ___ love to hear Dick Dale play. ___

Verse

3. Lis-ten to the king of the surf gui-tar. ___ Lis-ten to the king of the surf gui-tar. ___

Lis-ten, lis-ten to the king. _ Come on and

Outro

lis-ten. Come on and lis-ten. Come on and lis-ten. Come on and

Begin fade

lis-ten. Come on and lis-ten. Come on and lis-ten. Come on and

Fade out

lis-ten. Come on and lis-ten. Come on and lis-ten.

Let's Go Trippin'

By Dick Dale

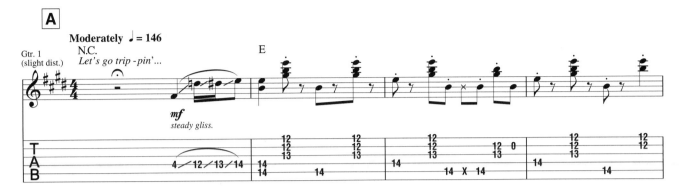

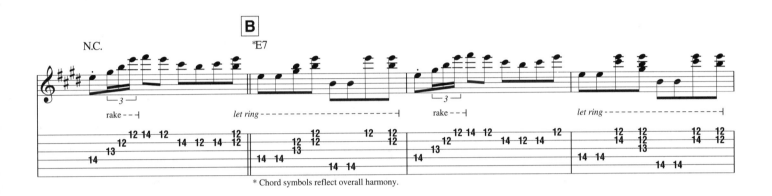

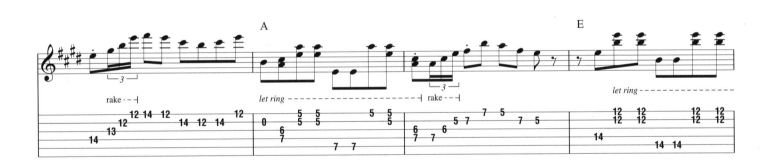

* Chord symbols reflect overall harmony.

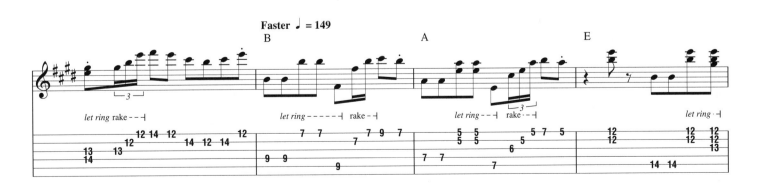

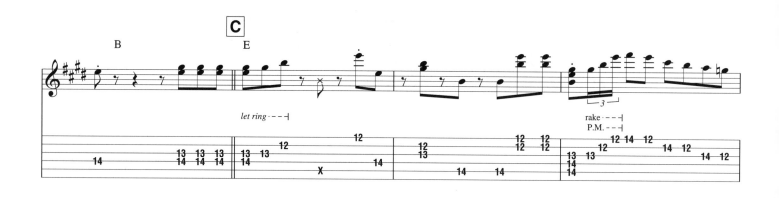

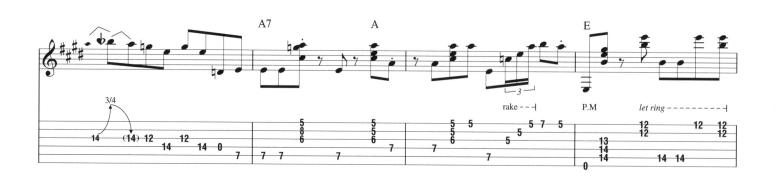

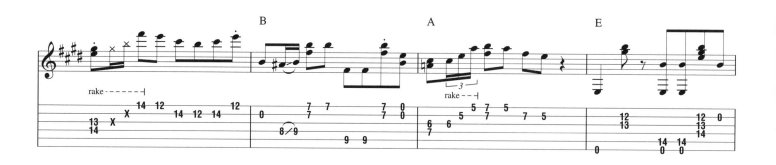

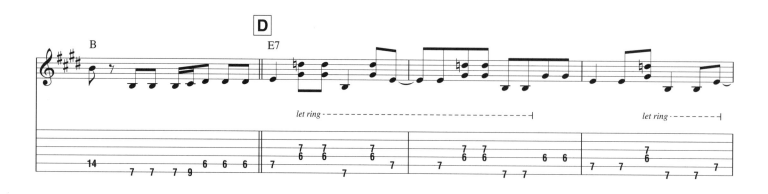

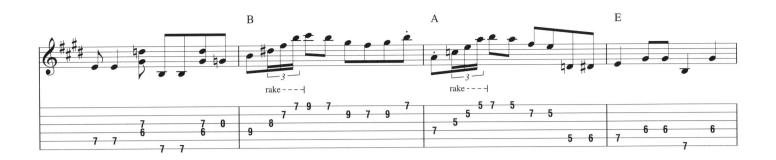

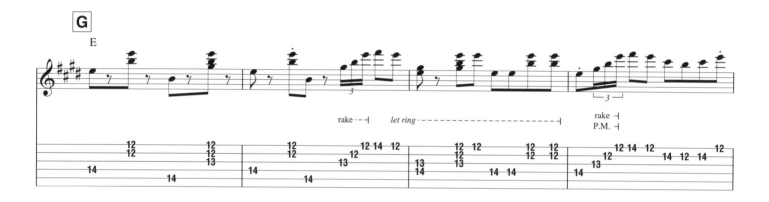

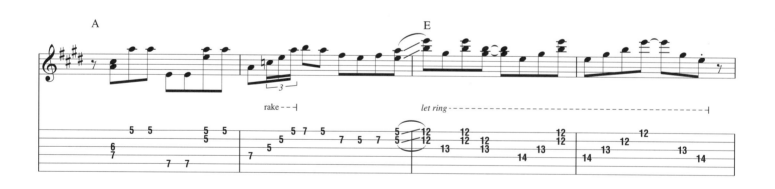

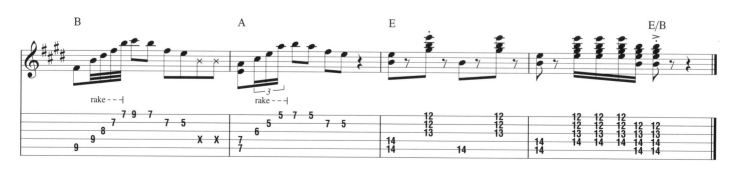

from *Better Shred Than Dead – The Dick Dale Anthology*

Misirlou

By Nicolas Roubanis

*Tremolo pick in sixteenth-note
pattern while sliding down string.

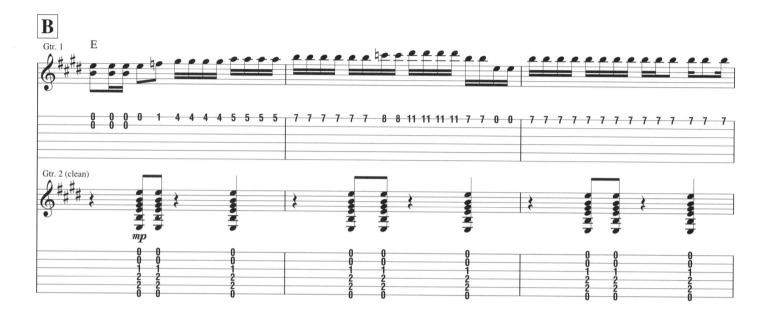

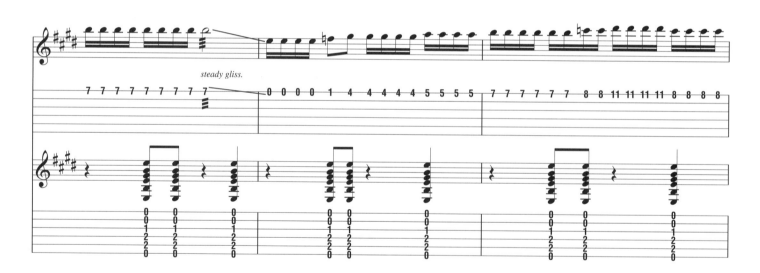

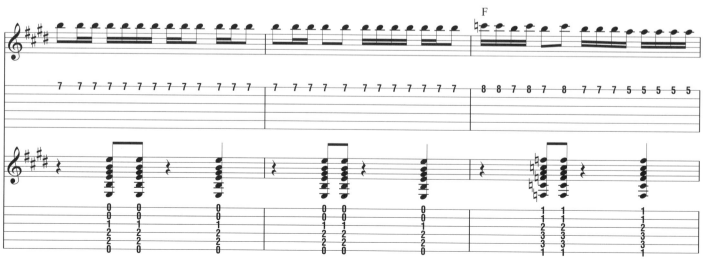

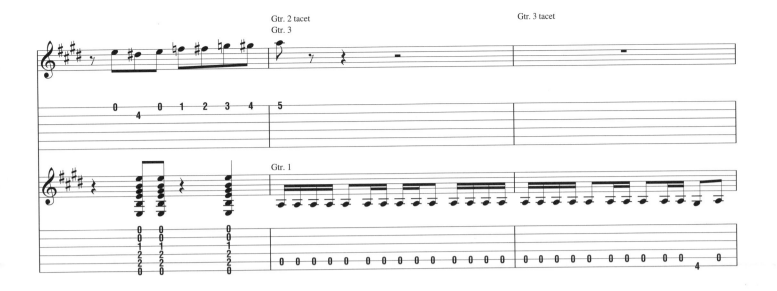

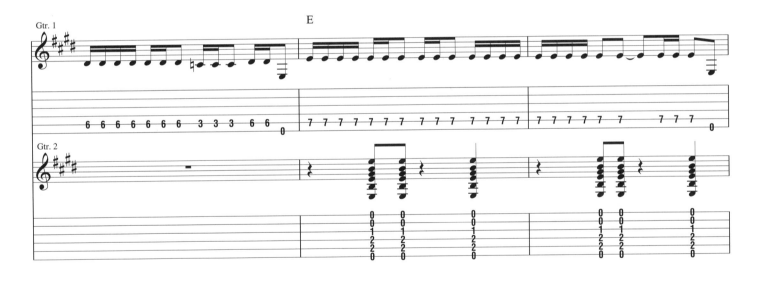

Play 5 times and fade

Night Rider

By Dick Dale

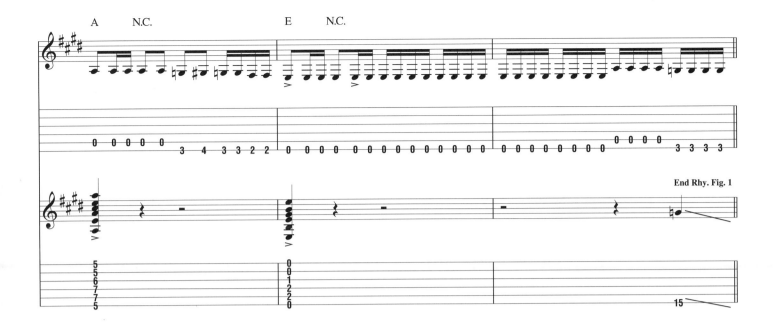

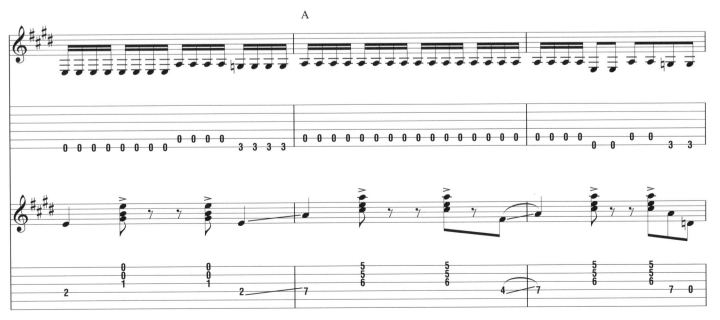

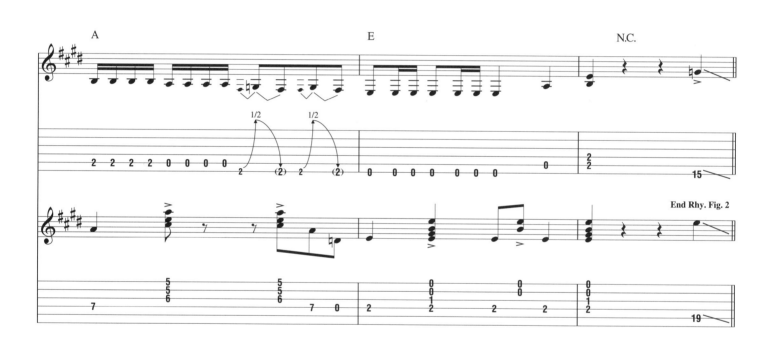

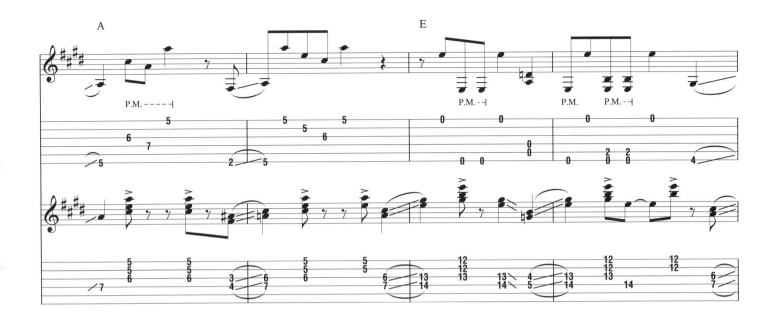

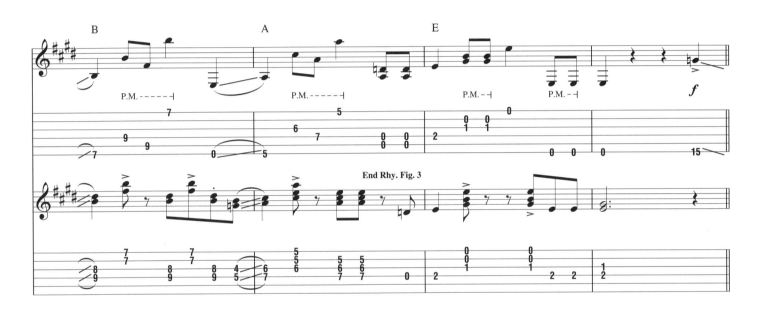

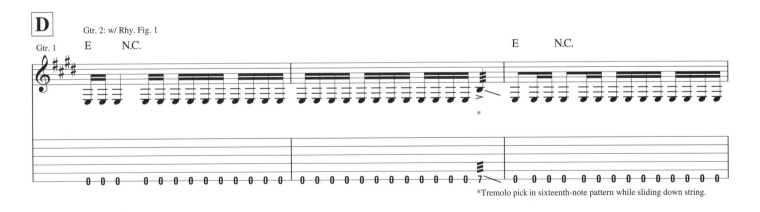

*Tremolo pick in sixteenth-note pattern while sliding down string.

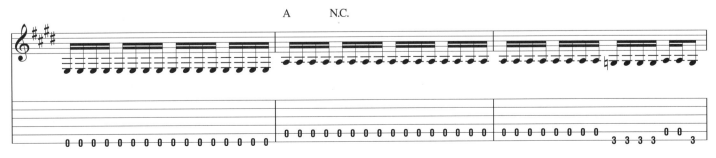

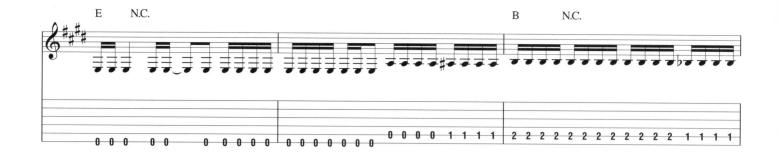

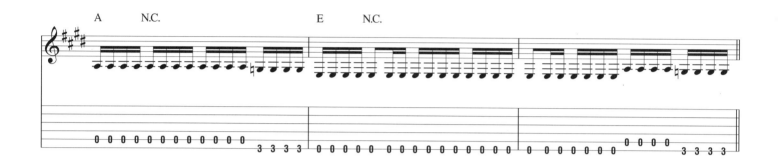

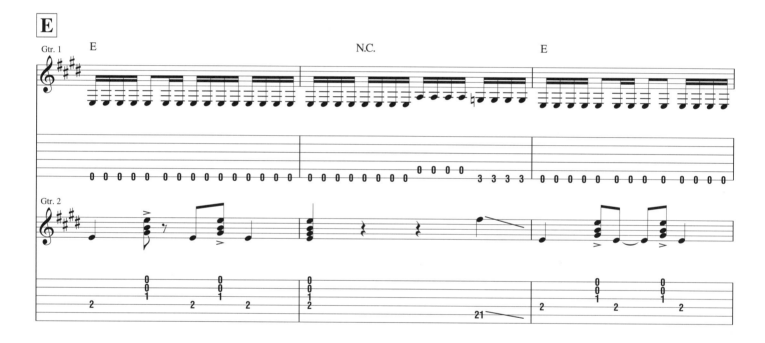

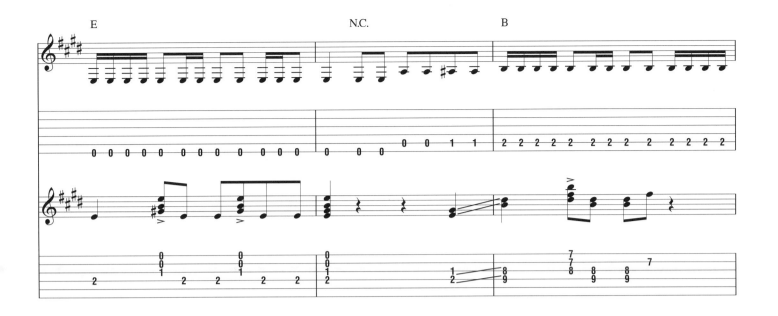

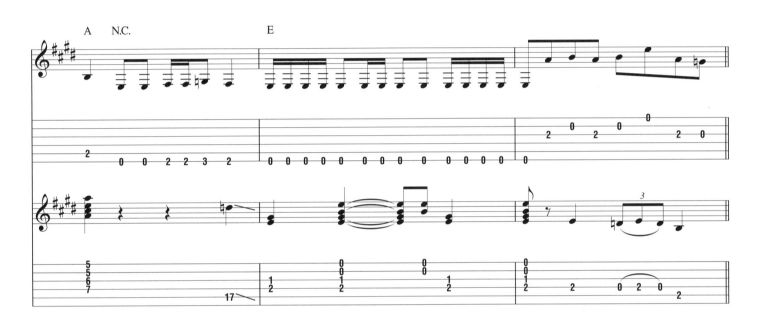

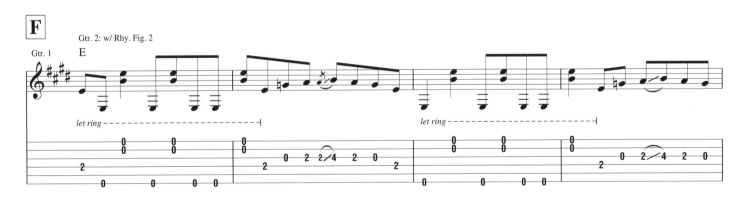

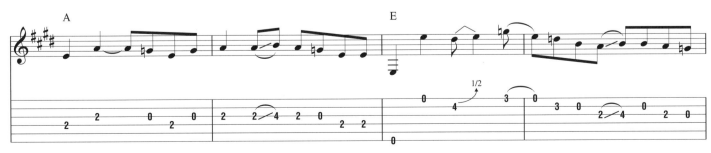

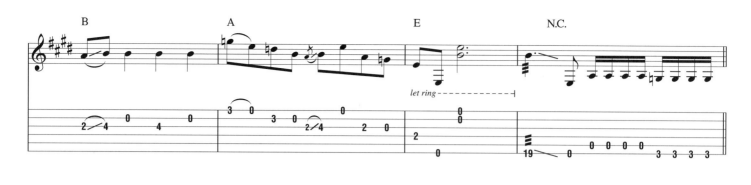

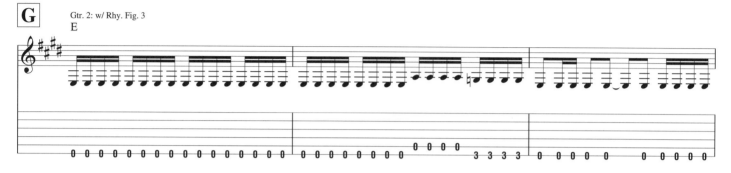

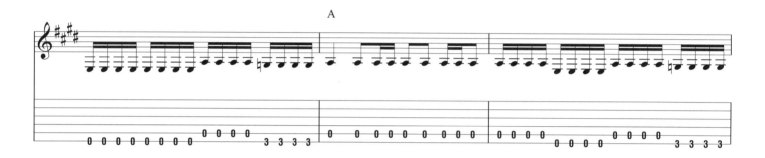

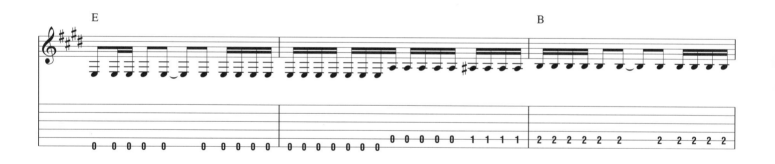

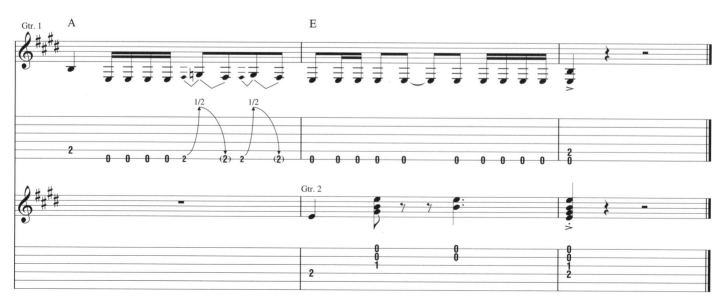

Nitro

By Dick Dale

*Chord symbols reflect implied harmony.

**Tremolo pick in sixteenth-note pattern while sliding down strings.

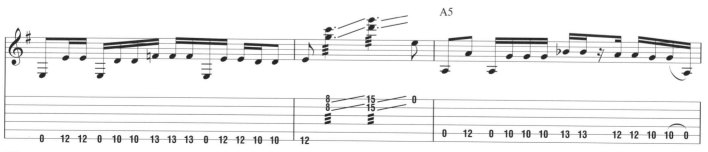

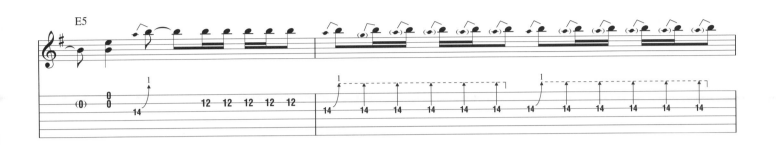

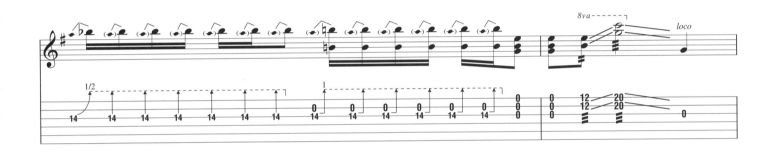

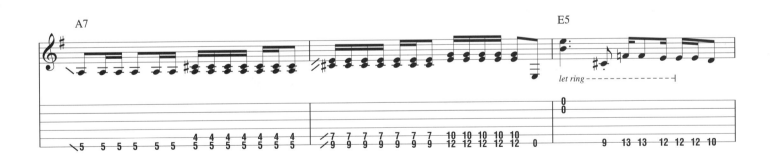

End double-time feel

*Picked as fast as possible.

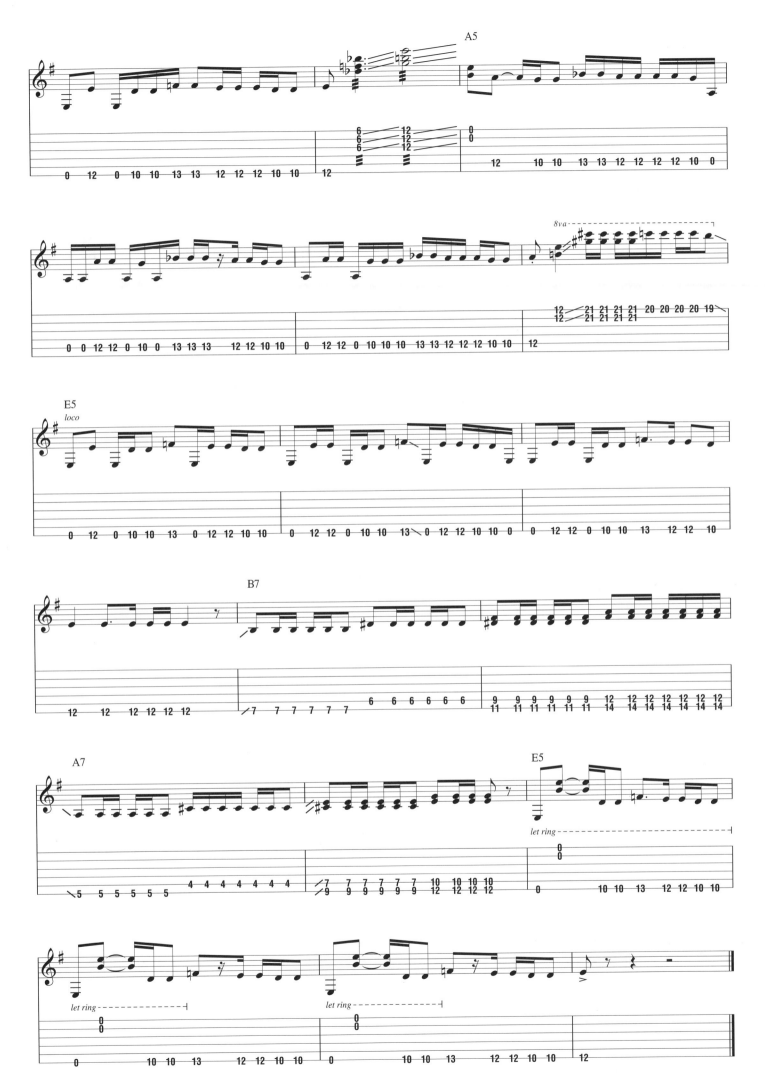

(Ghost) Riders in the Sky (A Cowboy Legend)

By Stan Jones

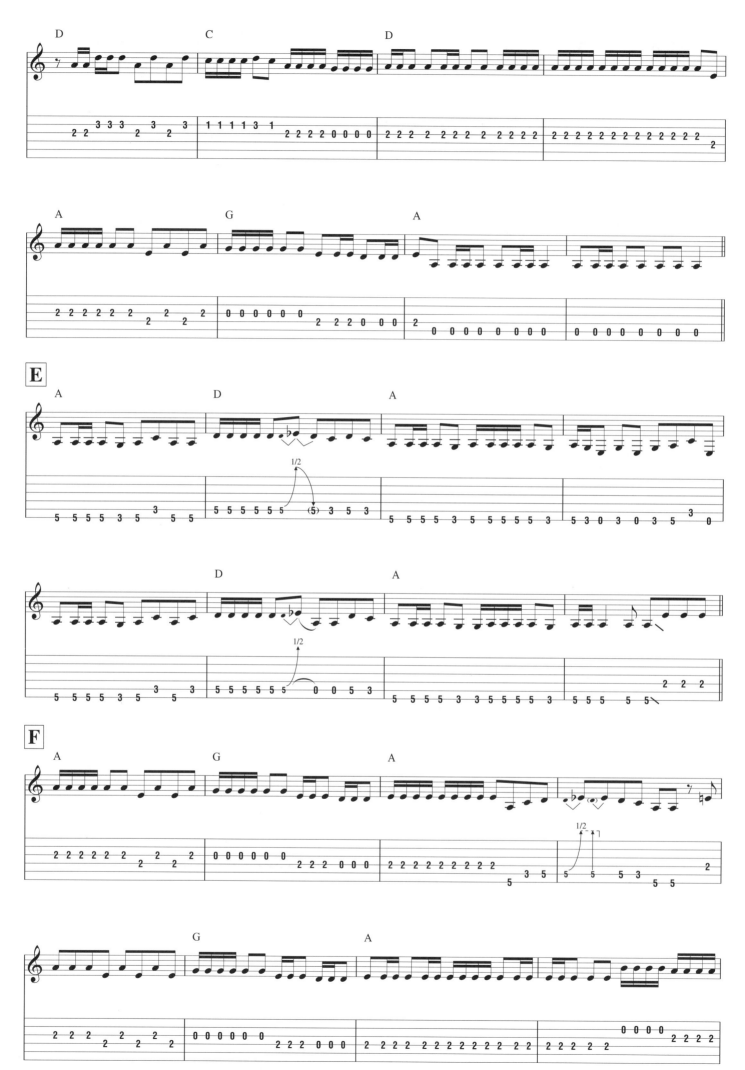

The Scavenger

Words and Music by Gary S. Paxton and William Paul Nuckles

D.S. al Coda

3. So, years

⊕ Coda

Outro

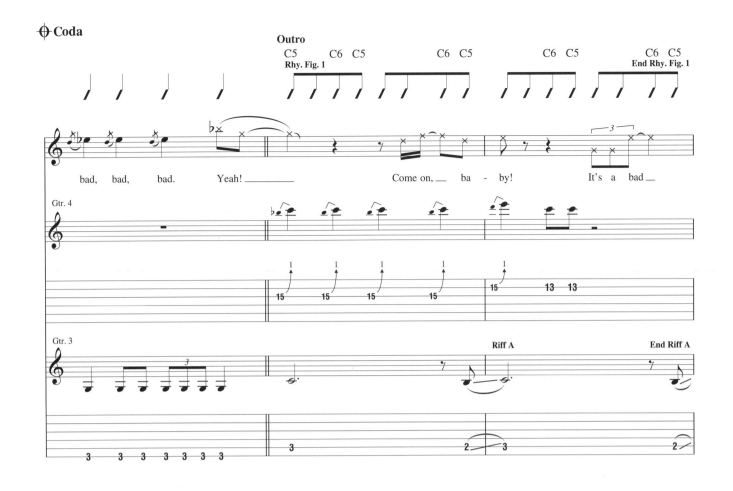

bad, bad, bad.   Yeah! _____   Come on, __ ba - by!   It's a bad __

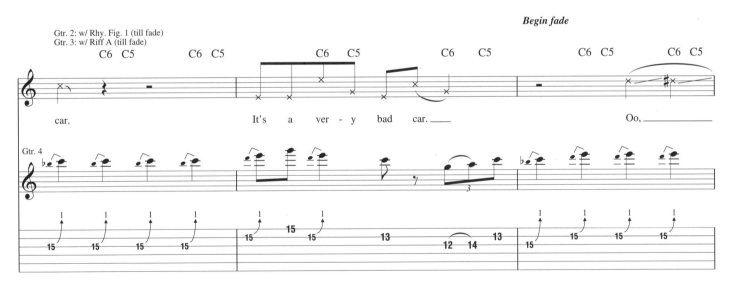

car.   It's a ver - y bad car. ___   Oo, _____

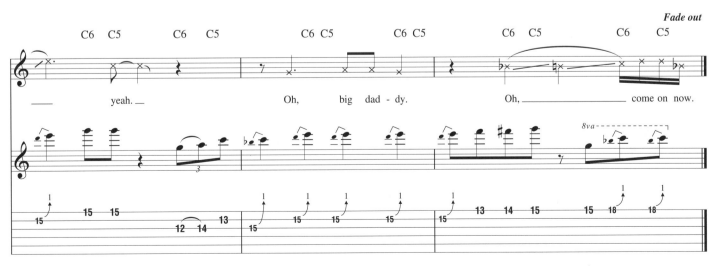

___   yeah. ___   Oh,   big dad - dy.   Oh, _____ come on now.

Shake 'n' Stomp

By Dick Dale

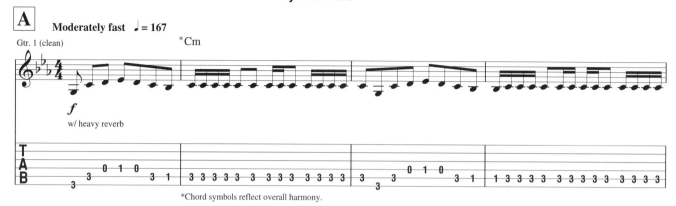

*Chord symbols reflect overall harmony.

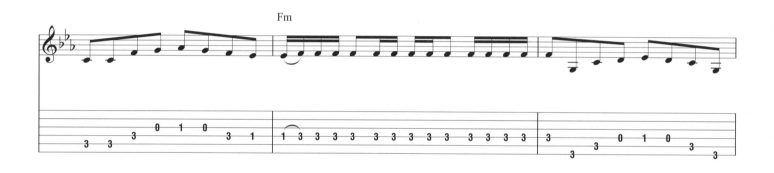

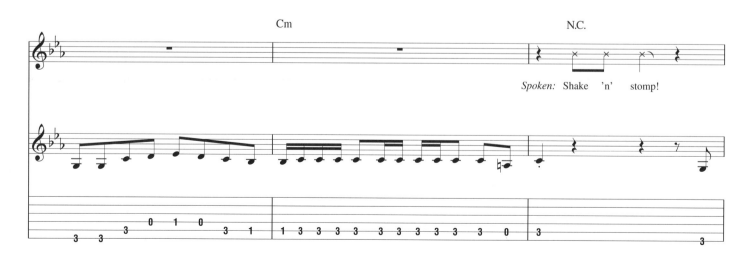

Spoken: Shake 'n' stomp!

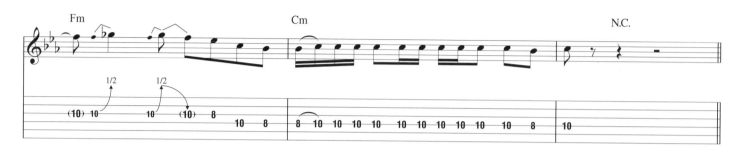

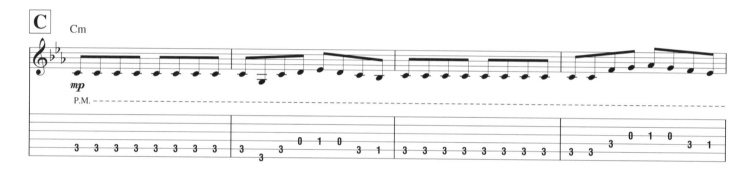

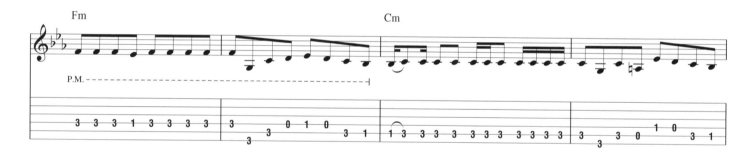

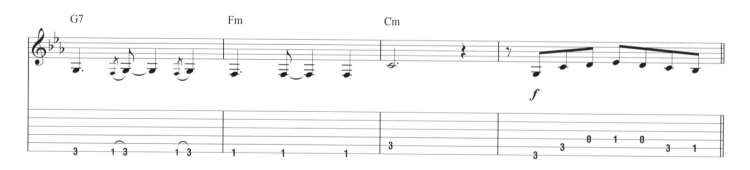

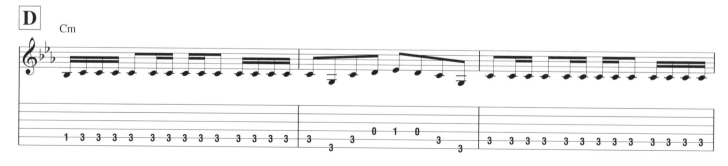

Surf Beat

By Dick Dale

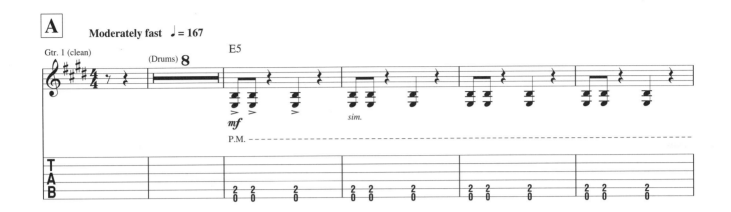

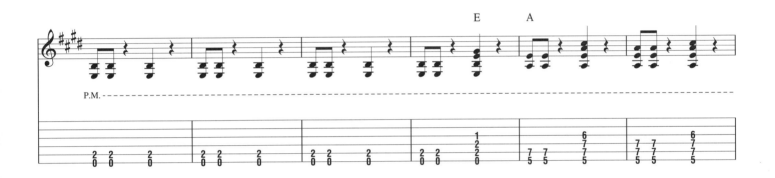

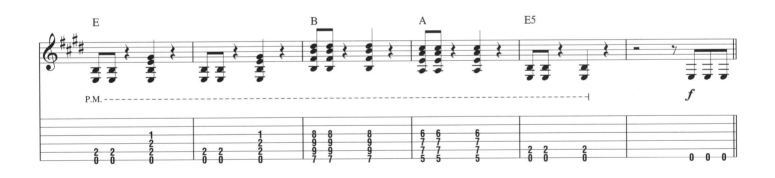

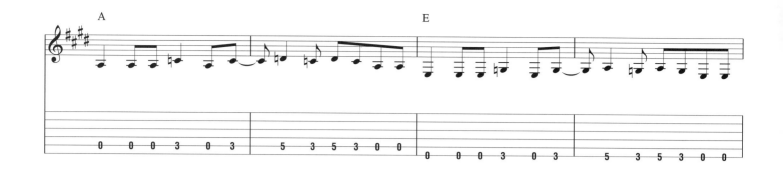

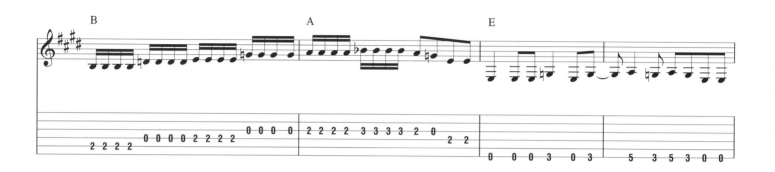

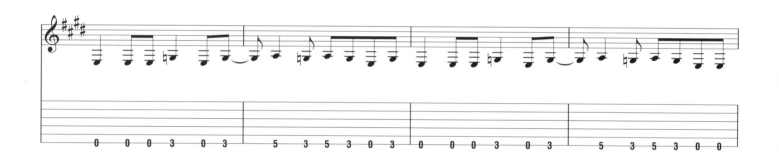

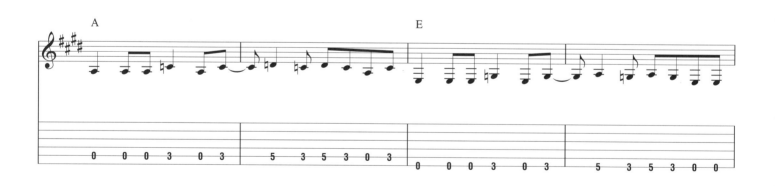

*Tremolo pick in
sixteenth-note pattern
while sliding down string.

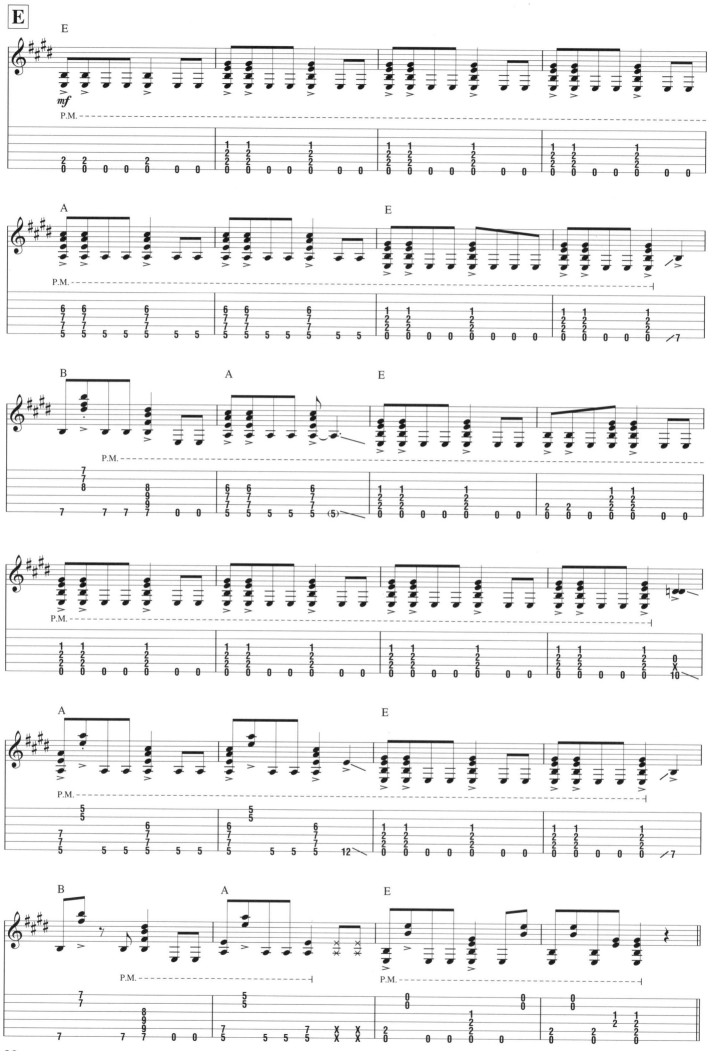